Bet and the Snake

Bet got a call at work.
"This is the police," said a voice.

The voice went on,
"Can you come? We need your help."

"I'll be there as soon as I can," said Bet.
"Come on, Jack. Into the van!"

Bet and Jack drove over to see the police.
They were waiting in an old block of flats.

Bet and Jack got out of the van.
A lot of people were waiting outside the flats.

Bet and Jack went into one of the flats.
A policewoman was waiting by a door.
"Look in there," she said.

Bet had a look. Behind the door was a snake. A very big snake!

Bet shut the door.
"We'll have to call the snakeman," she said.
"This snake is too big for us!"

Bet and the police waited for the snakeman to come. Jack did not like the snake. He kept growling.

The snakeman came to have a look.
" I hear it's a big one," he said.
"Let me have a look at it."

The snakeman opened the door and had a look.
"Wow! That is a big one!" he said.
"Who left it there?"

The snakeman put the snake into a big bag. "She'll be OK in there," he said.

The police helped the snakeman carry the bag down to the van. It was very heavy.

Later, Bet drove over to see how the snake was.
The snakeman had a snake home outside the town.

"The snake is OK," the snakeman told Bet.
"She's much better off here than in that flat!"

"What do you say to that, Jack?" said Bet.
Jack just growled.